Va

MW00744280

Quotes & Facts

By Blago Kirov

First Edition

*****

Van Gogh: Quotes & Facts
*****

Foreword

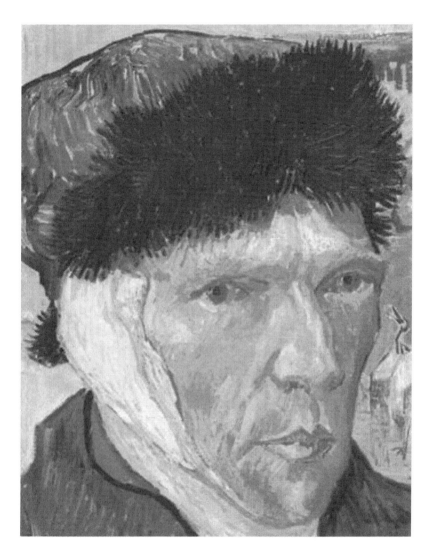

"Someday death will take us to another star."

This book is an anthology of 121 quotes from Vincent van Gogh and 50 selected facts about Vincent van Gogh.

A good picture is equivalent to a good deed.

Admire as much as you can. Most people do not admire enough.

An artist needn't be a clergyman or a church warden, but he must have a warm heart for his fellow men.

And sometimes there is relief, sometimes there is new inner energy, and one stands up after it; till at last, someday, one perhaps doesn't stand up any more, que soit, but that is nothing extraordinary, and I repeat, in my opinion, such is the common.

And then, I have nature and art and poetry, and if that is not enough, what is enough?

And when I read, and really I do not read so much, only a few authors, - a few men that I discovered by accident - I do this because they look at things in a broader, milder and more affectionate way than I do, and because they know life better, so that I can learn from them.

Art is to console those who are broken by life.

As we advance in life it becomes more and more difficult, but in fighting the difficulties the inmost strength of the heart is developed.

At present I absolutely want to paint a starry sky. It often seems to me that night is still more richly coloured than the day; having hues of the most intense violets, blues and greens. If only you pay attention to it you will see that certain stars are lemon-yellow, others pink or a green, blue and forget-me-not brilliance. And without my expatiating on this theme it is obvious that putting little white dots on the blue-black is not enough to paint a starry sky.

As a child, Vincent was serious, silent and thoughtful. A girl named Margot Begemann who was his neighbor, fell in love with him but Van Gogh rejected her causing her to try to commit suicide.

From 1869 to 1876, Van Gogh worked for his Uncle Cent, an art dealer. He spent time in both London and Paris before being let go.

Van Gogh started to paint with oil paints in 1883.

Vincent van Gogh briefly worked as a supply teacher in Ramsgate, England.

Vincent created a total of 2000 pieces of art which included 900 paintings and 1100 sketches and pencil drawings.

Vincent van Gogh was a self-taught artist.

Van Gogh sold just one painting, The Red Vineyard, during his lifetime.

Van Gogh's most expensive painting, Portrait of Dr. Gachet, is valued at $148.6 million dollars.

Some Facts about Vincent van Gogh

As a child, Vincent was serious, silent and thoughtful.

A girl named Margot Begemann who was his neighbor, fell in love with him but Van Gogh rejected her causing her to try to commit suicide.

From 1869 to 1876, Van Gogh worked for his Uncle Cent, an art dealer. He spent time in both London and Paris before being let go.

Van Gogh started to paint with oil paints in 1883.

Vincent van Gogh briefly worked as a supply teacher in Ramsgate, England.

Vincent created a total of 2000 pieces of art which included 900 paintings and 1100 sketches and pencil drawings.

Vincent van Gogh was a self-taught artist.

Van Gogh sold just one painting, The Red Vineyard, during his lifetime.

Van Gogh's most expensive painting, Portrait of Dr. Gachet, is valued at $148.6 million dollars.

Vincent was named after his grandfather and stillborn brother who died a year earlier than Van Gogh's birth.

Vincent's father was Reverend Theodorus van Gogh.

Vincent had several siblings – a brother named Theodorus nicknamed Theo, another named Cor, and three sisters whose names were Elisabeth, Anna and Willemina.

Exactly one year before Vincent was born; a son was born to his parents and named Vincent Willem Van Gogh. Unfortunately, he was stillborn. The tiny body was buried at the church where Vincent's father worked. Every time Vincent went to church, he saw a grave with his name and birth date on it.

Vincent van Gogh suffered from temporal lobe epilepsy, hallucinations and mental illness.

Vincent van Gogh's earliest career aspiration was to be a pastor in the Dutch Reformed Church like his father. He was a missionary temporarily, but eventually gave in to pressure from his parents and gave up on the idea.

In 1869, Vincent van Gogh took his first job, working in the Hague branch of an international art dealing firm.

Vincent was famous for painting sunflowers as a subject matter.

Vincent's brother Theo died six months after Vincent and is buried next to him in Auvers, France.

In 1880, at the age of 27, Vincent van Gogh decided to become an artist.

Vincent van Gogh was known to drink absinthe, an alcoholic drink sourced from wormwood and known for its hallucinogenic effects. Absinthe caused problems such as lesions of the brain and erratic behavior, and is believed to be a primary factor in Van Gogh's mental decline.

Van Gogh spent several years as an evangelist, ministering to the working class. He was dismissed from ministry because he was overly enthusiastic to the point of being considered a fanatic.

Van Gogh was financially supported most of his life by his brother, Theo.

Vincent van Gogh attended an art school for a few months in Antwerp, in 1885, which was four years before his death.

During an epileptic seizure, Van Gogh attempted to attack his friend Paul Gauguin with an open razor.

Van Gogh painted 37 self-portraits.

More than one hundred and fifty psychiatrists have tried to diagnose the cause of Vincent van Gogh's illnesses and the diagnoses range from schizophrenia, porphyria, syphilis, bipolar disorder, and epilepsy.

Van Gogh's work began to shoot to fame eleven years after his death due to the diligence of his brother's wife.

When Van Gogh first began painting, he used peasants as models and later would paint flowers, landscapes and himself, mostly because he was too poor to pay the models.

Vincent's brother's wife collected Vincent's paintings and letters after his death and dedicated herself to getting his work the recognition it deserved.

In a short period of ten years Van Gogh made approximately 900 paintings.

Paul Gauguin came to Arles in 1888 and the two artists worked side by side. During this period Gauguin produced a portrait of Van Gogh.

During his stay in Auvers-sur-Oise, Van Gogh completed a painting a day for seventy days.

In 1888, in Arles (France), Van Gogh produced some his most famous works, such as Van Gogh's Chair, The Night Cafe, Starry Night Over the Rhone, and Still Life: Vase with Twelve Sunflowers.

Van Gogh signed most of his major paintings with his first name. Usually, an artist signed with initials or the last name. He was a Dutchman with a name easy for non-Dutch to spell but difficult to pronounce. "Van Gogh" is not pronounced "van go" or "van goff" but a sound difficult to reproduce in English spelling. The best approximation is "van hawkgh" to sound similarly to "cough."

Vincent van Gogh did not cut off his ear. He only cut off a small portion of his ear lobe.

Van Gogh was close friends with Paul Gauguin, another famous artist.

Van Gogh created his most famous work The Starry Night while staying in an asylum in Saint-Remy-de-Provence, France.

Vincent's earliest career aspiration was to be a pastor in the Dutch Reformed Church like his father.

Some of Van Gogh's best works are Japanese-themed and Pacific Island related.

Van Gogh wrote over 800 letters in his lifetime, the majority of them written to his brother and closest friend Theo.

Vincent would often speak of his brother in the highest regard and say a finer brother a man could never have.

Vincent shot himself in a wheat field in Auvers, France but did not die until 2 days later at the age of 37.

Today Vincent Van Gogh is one of the most famous artists in the world and his work changes hands for millions of dollars.

Van Gogh's last painting was of a man who was sitting down with his head in his hands as if he were depressed.

His brother Theo, said that Vincent's last words were
"La tristesse durera toujours" which means "the
sadness will last forever."

Van Gogh's painting Ires was sold for a $53.9 million.

The Portrait of Joseph Roulin which was painted by Van Gogh in 1889 and was sold in August 1989 by a private collector to the Museum of Modern Art New York, USA is another very expensive work of arts. This painting was sold at a price of $110 million.

Van Gogh's Portrait de I'artiste sans barbe was sold in November 1998 at a price $101.5 millions to the heirs of Jacques Koerfer.

His 1889 A Wheatfield with Cypresses was sold at $92 million dollars in May 1993 by Emil Georg Burhle.

His Words

A good picture is equivalent to a good deed.

Admire as much as you can. Most people do not admire enough.

An artist needn't be a clergyman or a church warden, but he must have a warm heart for his fellow men.

And sometimes there is relief, sometimes there is new inner energy, and one stands up after it; till at last, someday, one perhaps doesn't stand up any more, que soit, but that is nothing extraordinary, and I repeat, in my opinion, such is the common.
And then, I have nature and art and poetry, and if that is not enough, what is enough?

And when I read, and really I do not read so much, only a few authors, - a few men that I discovered by accident - I do this because they look at things in a broader, milder and more affectionate way than I do, and because they know life better, so that I can learn from them.

Art is to console those who are broken by life.

As we advance in life it becomes more and more difficult, but in fighting the difficulties the inmost strength of the heart is developed.

At present I absolutely want to paint a starry sky. It often seems to me that night is still more richly coloured than the day; having hues of the most intense violets, blues and greens. If only you pay attention to it you will see that certain stars are lemon-yellow, others pink or a green, blue and forget-me-not brilliance. And without my expatiating on this theme it is obvious that putting little white dots on the blue-black is not enough to paint a starry sky.

Be clearly aware of the stars and infinity on high. Then life seems almost enchanted after all.

Both she and I have grief enough and trouble enough, but as for regrets – neither of us have any.

But for one's health as you say, it is very necessary to work in the garden and see the flowers growing.

Christ alone, of all the philosophers, magicians, etc., has affirmed eternal life as the most important certainty, the infinity of time, the futility of death, the necessity and purpose of serenity and devotion. He lived serenely, as an artist greater than all other artists, scorning marble and clay and paint, working in the living flesh. In other words, this peerless artist, scarcely conceivable with the blunt instrument of our modern, nervous and obtuse brains, made neither statues nor paintings nor books. He maintained in no uncertain terms that he made ... living men, immortals.

Close friends are truly life's treasures. Sometimes they know us better than we know ourselves. With gentle honesty, they are there to guide and support us, to share our laughter and our tears. Their presence reminds us that we are never really alone.
Do not quench your inspiration and your imagination; do not become the slave of your model.

Don't lose heart if it's very difficult at times, everything will come out all right and nobody can in the beginning do as he wishes.

Exaggerate the essential, leave the obvious vague.

Fortunately for me, I know well enough what I want, and am basically utterly indifferent to the criticism that I work to hurriedly. In answer to that, I have done some things even more hurriedly theses last few days.

Future generations will probably be able to enlighten us on this very interesting subject, and then science itself — with all due respect — may reach conclusions that are more or less in keeping with Christ's sayings about the other half of our life.

Great things are not done by impulse, but by a series of small things brought together.

How rich art is, if one can only remember what one has seen, one is never empty of thoughts or truly lonely, never alone.

How right it is to love flowers and the greenery of pines and ivy and hawthorn hedges; they have been with us from the very beginning.

I always think that the best way to know God is to love many things.

I am always doing what I cannot do yet, in order to learn how to do it.

I am seeking, I am striving, I am in it with all my heart.

I am still far from being what I want to be, but with God's help I shall succeed.

I can't change the fact that my paintings don't sell. But the time will come when people will recognize that they are worth more than the value of the paints used in the picture.

I confess I do not know why, but looking at the stars always makes me dream.

I don't know anything with certainty, but seeing the stars makes me dream.

I dream my painting and I paint my dream.

I experience a period of frightening clarity in those moments when nature is so beautiful. I am no longer sure of myself, and the paintings appear as in a dream.

I feel such a creative force in me: I am convinced that there will be a time when, let us say, I will make something good every day , on a regular basis....I am doing my very best to make every effort because I am longing so much to make beautiful things. But beautiful things mean painstaking work, disappointment, and perseverance.

I have lost my soul into my work, and I have lost my mind in the process.

I have tried to express the idea that the café is a place where one can ruin oneself, go mad, or commit a crime.

I know well that healing comes-if one is brave-from within, through profound resignation to suffering and death, through the surrender of your own will and of your self-love. But that is of no use to me; I love to paint, to see people and things and everything that makes our life-artificial, if you like. Yes, real life would be a different thing, but I do not belong to that category of souls who are ready to live and also at any moment to suffer. I am everything but courageous in sorrow, and everything but patient when I am not feeling well, though I have rather a good deal of patience in keeping to my work.

I often think of you all, one cannot do what one wants in life. The more you feel attached to a spot, the more ruthlessly you are compelled to leave it, but the memories remain, and one remembers - as in a looking glass, darkly - one's absent friends.

I must continue to follow the path I take now. If I do nothing, if I study nothing, if I cease searching, then, woe is me, I am lost. That is how I look at it — keep going, keep going come what may. But what is your final goal, you may ask. That goal will become clearer; will emerge slowly but surely, much as the rough draught turns into a sketch, and the sketch into a painting through the serious work done on it, through the elaboration of the original vague idea and through the consolidation of the first fleeting and passing thought.

I often think that the night is more alive and more richly colored than the day.

I put my heart and soul into my work, and I have lost my mind in the process.

I shouldn't precisely have chosen madness if there had been any choice, but once such a thing has taken hold of you, you can't very well get out of it.

I think that I still have it in my heart someday to paint a bookshop with the front yellow and pink in the evening...like a light in the midst of the darkness.

I try more and more to be myself, caring relatively little whether people approve or disapprove.

I want to touch people with my art. I want them to say 'he feels deeply, he feels tenderly'.

I wanted to make people think of a totally different way of living from that which we, educated people, live. I would absolutely not want anyone to find it beautiful or good without a thought.

I will not live without love."

I wish they would take me as I am.

I work as diligently on my canvases as the laborers do in their fields.

I would rather die of passion than of boredom.

If I am worth anything later, I am worth something now. For wheat is wheat, even if people think it is a grass in the beginning.

If one feels the need of something grand, something infinite, something that makes one feel aware of God, one need not go far to find it. I think that I see something deeper, more infinite, more eternal than the ocean in the expression of the eyes of a little baby when it wakes in the morning and coos or laughs because it sees the sun shining on its cradle.

If one loves nature one finds beauty everywhere.

If you don't have a dog--at least one--there is not necessarily anything wrong with you, but there may be something wrong with your life.

If you hear a voice within you saying, "You are not a painter," then by all means paint - and that voice will be silenced.

If you truly love nature, you will find beauty everywhere.

If you work with love and intelligence, you develop a kind of armour against people's opinions, just because of the sincerity of your love for nature and art. Nature is also severe and, to put it that way, hard, but never deceives and always helps you to move forward.

I'm such Nobody.

In my view, I am often immensely rich, not in money, but (although just now perhaps not all the time) rich because I have found my metier, something I can devote myself to heart and soul and that gives inspiration and meaning to my life.

In spite of everything, I shall rise again; I will take up my pencil, which I have forsaken in my great discouragement, and I will go on with my drawing.

In the end we shall have had enough of cynicism, skepticism and humbug, and we shall want to live more musically.

It always strikes me, and it is very peculiar, that, whenever we see the image of indescribable and unutterable desolation — of loneliness, poverty, and misery, the end and extreme of things — the thought of God comes into one's mind.

It is a pity that, as one gradually gains experience, one loses one's youth.

It is good to love many things, for therein lies the true strength, and whosoever loves much performs much, and can accomplish much, and what is done in love is well done.

It is looking at things for a long time that ripens you and gives you a deeper meaning.

It is not only by one's impulses that one achieves greatness, but also by patiently filing away the steel wall that separates what one feels from what one is capable of doing.

It is only right and proper to be moved by the Bible, but present-day reality has so strong a hold over us that even when we try to imagine the past the minor events in our lives immediately wrench us out of our musings, and our own adventures throw us back irrevocably upon our personal feelings — joy, boredom, suffering, anger, or a smile.

It is with the reading of books the same as with looking at pictures; one must, without doubt, without hesitations, with assurance, admire what is beautiful.

It's better to have a gay life of it than to commit suicide.

Just slap anything on when you see a blank canvas staring you in the face like some imbecile. You don't know how paralyzing that is, that stare of a blank canvas is, which says to the painter, 'You can't do a thing'. The canvas has an idiotic stare and mesmerizes some painters so much that they turn into idiots themselves. Many painters are afraid in front of the blank canvas, but the blank canvas is afraid of the real, passionate painter who dares and who has broken the spell of `you can't' once and for all.

Keep your love of nature, for that is the true way to understand art more and more.

Let me stop there, but my God, how beautiful Shakespeare is, who else is as mysterious as he is; his language and method are like a brush trembling with excitement and ecstasy. But one must learn to read, just as one must learn to see and learn to live.

Let us keep courage and try to be patient and gentle. And let us not mind being eccentric, and make distinction between good and evil.

Let's not forget that the little emotions are the great captains of our lives and we obey them without realizing it.

Life itself, too, is forever turning an infinitely vacant, dispiriting blank side towards man on which nothing appears, any more than it does on a blank canvas. But no matter how vacant and vain, how dead life may appear to be, the man of faith, of energy, of warmth, who knows something, will not be put off so easily.

Love is eternal -- the aspect may change, but not the essence. There is the same difference in a person before and after he is in love as there is in an unlighted lamp and one that is burning. The lamp was there and was a good lamp, but now it is shedding light too, and that is its real function. And love makes one calmer about many things, and that way, one is more fit for one's work.

Modern reality has got such a hold on us that... when we attempt to reconstruct the ancient days in our thoughts...the minor events of our lives tear us away from our meditations, and... thrust us back into our personal problems.

Normality is a paved road: It's comfortable to walk, but no flowers grow on it.

One begins by plaguing oneself to no purpose in order to be true to nature, and one concludes by working quietly from one's own palette alone, and then nature is the result.

One may have a blazing hearth in one's soul and yet no one ever came to sit by it. Passers-by see only a wisp of smoke from the chimney and continue on their way.

One must work and dare if one really wants to live.

Only when I fall do I get up again.

Our goals can only be reached through a vehicle of a plan, in which we must fervently believe, and upon which we must vigorously act. There is no other route to success."

Quick work doesn't mean less serious work, it depends on one's self-confidence and experience. In the same way Jules Guérard, the lion hunter, says in his book that in the beginning young lions have a lot of trouble killing a horse or an ox, but that the old lions kill with a single blow of the paw or a well-placed bite, and that they are amazingly sure at the job... I must warn you that everyone will think that I work too fast. Don't you believe a word of it. Is it not emotion, the sincerity of one's feeling for nature, that draws us, and if the emotions are sometimes so strong that one works without knowing one works, when sometimes the strokes come with a continuity and coherence like words in a speech or a letter, then one must remember that it has not always been so, and that in time to come there will again be hard days, empty of inspiration. So one must strike while the iron is hot, and put the forged bars on one side.

Seek only light and freedom and do not immerse yourself too deeply in the worldly mire.

Someday death will take us to another star.

Sometimes, dear brother, I know so well what I want. I am quite able to do without God, both in my life and in my painting, but what I cannot do without, unwell as I am, is something greater than myself, which is my life, the power to create.

Success is sometimes the outcome of a whole string of failures.

That I was not suited to commerce or academic study in no way proves that I should also be unfit to be a painter.

The beginning is perhaps more difficult than anything else, but keep heart, it will turn out all right.

The best way to know God is to love many things.

The best way to know life is to love many things.

The cure for him would be to take a good long look at some potato plants, which have lately had such a deep and distinctive colour and tone, instead of driving himself mad looking at pieces of yellow satin and gold leather.

The fishermen know that the sea is dangerous and the storm terrible, but they have never found these dangers sufficient reason for remaining ashore.

The heart of man is very much like the sea, it has its storms, it has its tides and in its depths it has its pearls too.

The lamps are burning and the starry sky is over it all.

The more ugly, old, nasty, ill, and poor I become the more I want to get my own back by producing vibrant, well-arranged, radiant colour.

The only time I feel alive is when I'm painting.

The sadness will last forever.

The sunflower is mine, in a way.

The victory one would gain after a whole life of work and effort is better than one that is gained sooner.

The world concerns me only in so far as I have a certain debt and duty to it, because I have lived in it for thirty years and owe to it to leave behind some souvenir in the shape of drawings and paintings – not done to please any particular movement, but within which a genuine human sentiment is expressed.

There are two ways of reasoning about painting: how to do it and how not to do it; how to d it with great deal of drawing and not much colour, how not to do it with a great deal of colour and not much drawing.

There is but one Paris and however hard living may be here, and if it became worse and harder even — the French air clears up the brain and does good — a world of good.

There is nothing more truly artistic than to love people.

There is peace even in the storm.

There may be a great fire in our soul, yet no one ever comes to warm himself at it, and the passers-by see only a wisp of smoke.

There was a sentence in your letter that struck me, "I wish I were far away from everything, I am the cause of all, and bring only sorrow to everybody, I alone have brought all this misery on myself and others." These words struck me because that same feeling, just the same, not more nor less, is also on my conscience.

Those who dream by day are cognizant of many things which escape those who dream only by night.

To look at the stars always makes me dream, as simply as I dream over the black dots of a map representing towns and villages. Why, I ask myself, should the shining dots of the sky not be as accessible as the black dots on the map of France?

To suffer without complaint is the only lesson we have to learn in this life.

We feel lonely now and then and long for friends and think we should be quite different and happier if we found a friend of whom we might say: "He is the one." But you, too, will begin to learn that there is much self-deception behind this longing; if we yielded too much to it, it would lead us from the road.

Well, right now it seems that things are going very badly for me, have been doing so for some considerable time, and may continue to do so well into the future. But it is possible that everything will get better after it has all seemed to go wrong. I am not counting on it, it may never happen, but if there should be a change for the better I should regard that as a gain, I should rejoice, I should say, at last! So there was something after all!

What am I in the eyes of most people — a nonentity, an eccentric, or an unpleasant person — somebody who has no position in society and will never have; in short, the lowest of the low. All right, then — even if that were absolutely true, then I should one day like to show by my work what such an eccentric, such a nobody, has in his heart. That is my ambition, based less on resentment than on love in spite of everything, based more on a feeling of serenity than on passion. Though I am often in the depths of misery, there is still calmness, pure harmony and music inside me. I see paintings or drawings in the poorest cottages, in the dirtiest corners. And my mind is driven towards these things with an irresistible momentum.

What color is in a picture, enthusiasm is in life.

What is done in love is done well.

What preys on my mind is simply this one question: what am I good for, could I not be of service or use in some way?

What would life be if we had no courage to attempt anything?

When I have a terrible need of - shall I say the word - religion, then I go out and paint the stars.

When I see how several painters I know here are struggling with their watercolours and paintings so that they can't see a solution anymore, I sometimes think: Friend, the fault is in your drawing. I don't regret for a moment that I did not go in for watercolour and oil painting straight away. I am sure I will catch up if only I struggle on, so that my hand does not waver in drawing and perspective.

Whoever loves much, performs much, and can accomplish much, and what is done in love is done well.

Your profession is not what brings home your weekly paycheck, your profession is what you're put here on earth to do, with such passion and such intensity that it becomes spiritual in calling.

To do good work one must eat well, be well housed, have one's fling from time to time, smoke one's pipe, and drink one's coffee in peace.

Made in United States
Orlando, FL
30 October 2023

38394867R00021